THE GALLOPING HOUR: FRENCH POEMS

ALSO BY ALEJANDRA PIZARNIK

A Musical Hell
Extracting the Stone of Madness: Poems 1962–1972

THE GALLOPING HOUR: FRENCH POEMS

ALEJANDRA PIZARNIK

EDITED, WITH AN INTRODUCTION, BY PATRICIO FERRARI

TRANSLATED BY PATRICIO FERRARI AND FORREST GANDER

A New Directions Paperbook Original

Further notes on the text and images can be found on the New Directions website: https://ndbooks.com/gallopinghour.

Manufactured in the United States of America
First published as New Directions Paperbook 1414 in 2018

Library of Congress Cataloging-in-Publication Data
Names: Pizarnik, Alejandra, 1936–1972 author. | Ferrari, Patricio editor translator. | Gander, Forrest, 1956– translator.
Title: *The galloping hour : French poems* / Alejandra Pizarnik ; edited, with an introduction, by Patricio Ferrari ; translated by Patricio Ferrari and Forrest Gander.
Description: First edition. | New York : New Directions Publishing, 2018. | Includes bibliographical references.
Identifiers: LCCN 2018006022 (print) | LCCN 2018002151 (ebook) | ISBN 9780811227759 (ebook) | ISBN 9780811227742 (alk. paper)
Classification: LCC PQ7797.P576 (print) | LCC PQ7797.P576 A2 2018 (ebook) | DDC 841/.914--dc23
LC record available at https://lccn.loc.gov/2018006022

10 9 8 7 6 5 4 3

New Directions Books are published for James Laughlin
by New Directions Publishing Corporation
80 Eighth Avenue, New York 10011

ndbooks.com

CONTENTS

III. ANNEXES

INTRODUCTION

> Hay, madre, un sitio en el mundo, que se llama París.
> Un sitio muy grande y lejano y otra vez grande.[1]
>
> (There is, mother, a place in the world called Paris.
> A very big place and far and very big again.)
>
> – César Vallejo

In a diary entry of May 1959, while still living with her parents in Buenos Aires, shortly after the publication of her third poetry collection, the twenty-three-year-old Alejandra Pizarnik wrote:

> Je voudrais vivre pour écrire. Non penser à autre chose qu'à écrire. Je ne prétend [*sic*] pas l'amour ni l'argent. Je ne veux pas penser, ni construire décemment ma vie. Je veux de la paix: lire, étudier, gagner un peu d'argent pour m'independiser [sic] de ma famille, et écrire.[2]
>
> (I would like to live in order to write. Not to think of anything else other than to write. I am not after love nor money. I don't want to think nor decently build my life. I want peace: to read, to study, to earn some money so that I become independent from my family, and to write.)

Bold and assertive in tone, these words are less of a confession than a daring conviction, a resolution, a literary plan. Circumstantial? Purposely stylized? Perhaps the more essential question here is: Why did the Argentinian-born poet turn to a foreign language that, until then, she'd almost exclusively employed just to read French literature?

The younger of two daughters to Jewish immigrants who settled in Argentina during the 1930s, Flora Alejandra Pizarnik was born on April 29, 1936, in Avellaneda – a port city located within the greater Buenos Aires metropolitan area. Her parents, Ela Pizarnik and Rejzla Bromiker de Pizarnik, had left Równe, then part of Poland, two years earlier to flee the rising wave of antisemitism across Eastern Europe.[3] The family spoke Yiddish and Spanish at home, and the two sisters, Myriam and Alejandra, attended a progressive Jewish school. Alejandra grew up among these two languages, along with the accepted Latin American notion of French – of France – as inseparable from high culture, especially for those with fine-art or literary aspirations.

After Pizarnik sketched out a literary plan, in the same spiral-bound gray Avon notebook, she noted:

> Tengo que ir a Francia. *Recordarlo.* Recordar que debo quererlo mucho. Recordar que es lo único que me queda por querer, en este mundo ancho y alto.[4]
>
> (I have to go to France. *Remember it.* Remember that I must want it badly. Remember that this is the only thing left to want, in this world wide and deep.)

Not many today would disagree that this "obligation" resulted from a condition, partially elective, partially brought on by historical pressures. A quick glance at the biographies of some of the great European and North and Latin American writers of the past century reveals, more often than not, a single beacon, a common destination – one unrivaled city, sought after for its bohemian cultural scene.

By the early 1920s, with literary modernism at its apogee, Paris was the creative center of the western world, with Ezra Pound, James Joyce, and César Vallejo, to name but three, among the many foreign authors who took up residence there. The list is extensive. Some even abandoned their mother tongue and made French their writing language, as is the case of Vallejo's compatriot César Moro, or, in the late thirties, the Romanian philosopher Emil Cioran – one of the finest prose writers of the twentieth century in French.

Paris lured the rich and the poor, the established and the aspiring, the singular and uninspired.

Within a few decades, the City of Light had become home to a large community of expatriate authors and artists from around the globe. The French capital and, to some extent, the genius of the French language came to be equated with a rite of passage – the grand yet tangible myth.

In the aftermath of World War II, the heart of Paris welcomed those Latin American writers associated with the Boom and Post-Boom (Julio Cortázar, Mario Vargas Llosa, Severo Sarduy), as well as many nomadic writer-diplomats hailing from the other side of the Atlantic (Miguel Ángel Asturias, Octavio Paz, Alejo Carpentier). By this time, a surrealist poetic current had spread across the New World; in Argentina, it circulated among a second generation of avant-garde Francophile artists and poets, including the Spanish painter Juan Batlle Planas (in whose atelier the young Alejandra Pizarnik briefly studied after dropping out of the University of Buenos Aires), the poet-painter Enrique Molina, and the poet Olga Orozco – all of whom were friends with Pizarnik by the late 1950s.[5]

Increasingly obsessed with her craft and her literary image, and encouraged by close friends, Pizarnik, who had relatives in France, became part of the draw of Paris. On March 11, 1960, without professional obligations or any real responsibilities, she embarked on the transatlantic *Laenec*. Not for a movement. Not for any theoretical school, but on a self-imposed literary exile. She departed for a city that was not the cultural museum it is today (many chose to live there with moderate or meager means). She left for Paris – so big and vibrant and beautiful.

In the first few months, however, Pizarnik lived on the margins of the dreamed city. She arrived in the western suburbs, initially lodging in Châtenay-Malabry with one of her paternal uncles; then in Neuilly-sur-Seine with another one of her father's brothers. Both were Jewish immigrants who had been forced to escape their native

Poland three decades prior. Disappointed and dissatisfied, Alejandra knew she hadn't come to Paris just to duplicate her ordinary life in Buenos Aires.

Despite this situation, Pizarnik was not deterred. A poetic vision sustained her, and rapidly, through a kaleidoscope of literary references and landmarks, Alejandra embraced a quotidian existence inextricable from literature: under the iron footbridge where La Maga, muse of Cortázar's best-known novel, *Hopscotch*, and the author himself kept running into each other a decade earlier; at the cafés on the boulevards Saint-Germain-des-Prés and Saint-Michel; or by the Seine where booksellers of used and antiquarian books plied their trade. She walked the streets, seeing and hearing them, loving what she witnessed. Here, during the next four years, she met surrealist figures (Georges Bataille, Jean Arp, Max Ernst), befriended and translated some of the most notable French writers of her day (André Pieyre de Mandiargues, Henri Michaux, Yves Bonnefoy), wrote, and, most significantly, read and reread (in Spanish and French) a wide range of authors across genres and traditions.[6]

Pain, late night perambulations, and poverty – Pizarnik believed these were the roots of lasting art. She gambled her health and well-being against her poetry and the mysteries of language. Yet she longed for family and friends in Buenos Aires. Her native Buenos Aires represented her immature self – as Pizarnik relates in a diary entry on January 11, 1961. This weighed on her; however, she chose not to retreat, despite financial constraints, self-doubt, periods of debilitating mental health, and a fear of going mad.

The first two years of her Paris sojourn were erratic. Still unknown as a poet, Pizarnik changed her address at least five times. Only in 1962 did she find some respite, a place permanent enough to focus on what actually mattered. She moved to a fourth-floor attic room at 30 rue Saint-Sulpice, facing the back of the seventeenth-century Roman Catholic Church where Delacroix's *La Lutte de Jacob avec l'Ange* still adorns one of its walls. Ivonne Bordelois, then a student at the Sorbonne and one of Alejandra's closest compatriots in Paris, describes this space as

> Rimbaud's drunken boat, a zone of intense tobacco and the prodigious disorder of books and papers, a nomad's shop where a samovar dominated, and that special atmosphere that grows in the places where silence also grows, like an invading honeysuckle, nocturnal, permanent; the silence and a static, vibrant concentration, where the voice of Alejandra was queen.[7]

This was Pizarnik's most productive period, the year of *Árbol de Diana* (*Diana's Tree*) – her fourth poetry collection, accompanied with a celebratory preface by her friend and the future Nobel Prize winner Octavio Paz. Published in December of 1962 in Buenos Aires, this book of poems and prose poems in Spanish granted her immediate entry into the pantheon of Latin American poetry. It was a turning point also in form and style. The brevity of the texts suggested the impersonal, the anonymous, yet strangely radiated an aura of nocturnal intimacy. The myth of Pizarnik the Pythia, the poet priestess, the visionary, was set forth. Sensual and oblique, meticulous, allusive, in the modernist vein, *Árbol de Diana* presented a ruptured lyrical subject:

> Miedo de ser dos
> camino del espejo
>
> (Fear of being two
> path of the mirror)

This shattering image of self is traceable to a sentence that Pizarnik originally conceived in French while in Paris: "J'aurai aimé me voir dans une autre nuit, hors du délire d'être deux chemins du miroir" ("How I would have loved to see myself in some other night, beyond this madness of being two sides of the mirror"), found in "Paroles du vent" ("Words of the wind"), one of the texts collected in *The Galloping Hour*.

Alejandra's breakthrough *Árbol de Diana* and her experiments in French are contemporaneous – dating mostly from 1962, while she lived in that small space not far from the Latin Quarter. She arranged the latter writings under the generic heading "poemas franceses" – an inscription scrawled on a page torn from a copy of *Chemins de surréalisme* (Paths of surrealism) by the Franco-American art critic and historian Patrick Waldberg.

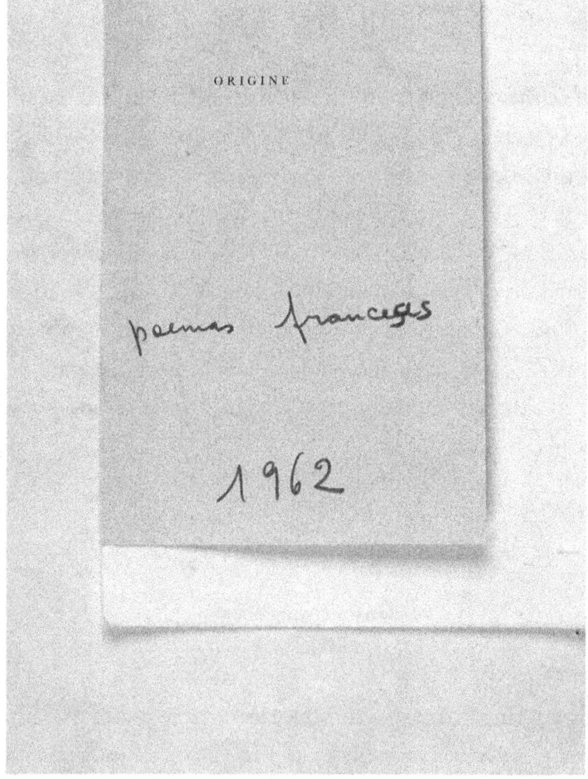

When Pizarnik returned to Buenos Aires, she almost never wrote in French again. Some of the French texts, however, were not forgotten, as a diary entry dated June 2, 1967, attests: "*Libro*: ver poemas viejos. *Phrases*. Traducir poemas en prosa franceses." ("*Book*: see old poems. *Phrases*. Translate French prose poems".) "Libro" may have referred to *Extracción de la piedra de locura* (*Extracting the Stone of Madness*), her fifth poetry collection, published in Buenos Aires the following year. Interestingly, lines from two of its poems are also traceable to passages now in *The Galloping Hour*. In fact, nearly a dozen Spanish texts included in books from *Árbol de Diana* to *El infierno musical* (*A Musical Hell*) (1971), and the posthumous *Textos de sombra y ultimos poemas* (Shadow texts and last poems) (1982) contain passages that Pizarnik first wrote in French and later translated into Spanish.[8]

Written by hand on loose papers probably without publication in mind, these French texts explore many of Pizarnik's deepest obsessions: the limitation of language, silence, the body, night, the nature of intimacy, madness, death. She was obsessed with the in-between, with the lyrical subject between cultures and between languages; she explored both sides of the mirror. These obsessions continued to haunt Pizarnik for the next decade, until her tragic death on September 25, 1972.

The Galloping Hour gathers for the first time, and in English, all the poems and prose poems the Argentinian-born poet produced in French. (The book's title is not by Pizarnik; it is taken from her poem "Words of the wind.") While Part I includes the "poemas franceses," Part II comprises those texts found outside this nucleus, scattered in different parts of the Pizarnik archive. Part III concludes with Pizarnik's verbal artwork: eight French-titled drawings in green marker and an etching with French prose text.[9] For the final versions of the texts, I systematically opted for the author's last version (in case of multiple ones) and her last signed intervention (in case of variants). When deemed necessary, I've corrected the orthography and/or syntax. Since this is not a critical edition, neither signed variants nor editorial interventions are indicated in the notes. Punctuation of the original texts has not been altered. This edition includes facsimiles of all twenty-eight documents from the Alejandra Pizarnik Papers held at Princeton University.[10] Further notes on the text and images can be found on the New Directions website at https://ndbooks.com/gallopinghour.

When Alejandra committed suicide by overdosing on Seconal at the age of thirty-six, in her Buenos Aires apartment on Montevideo Street, she left to posterity one of the most unusual bodies of work in Latin American literature. It is a body that includes a significant number of unpublished manuscripts, typescripts, and notebooks, containing poems, prose poems, fiction, diaries, fragments, reading notes, drawings.

Like that of the great Fernando Pessoa (a key figure in European modernism recently published by New Directions, whose posthumous works are still being discovered at the National Library of Portugal), the Pizarnik archive contains hidden and scattered treasures. There are scores of creative texts, visual works, and biographical information available to anyone willing to make the journey to Princeton.

I first visited the archive in the spring of 2009. I was then residing in Lisbon, reading Pessoa intensively. For the next nine years I would return to read Pizarnik: Pizarnik at work, the untold Pizarnik. (Like Pessoa, the author Alejandra Pizarnik quoted other works in various notebooks.) Alejandra's atelier of work is nowhere more present than in the papers – in the life of the papers. And now here in the present of this *Galloping Hour*.

1. Opening of Vallejo's "El buen sentido" ("The Good Sense"), published in *Poemas Humanos* (1939) a year after the poet's death. Pizarnik wrote this quote in a notebook she kept during 1970–1971.

2. Entry written May 8–19, 1959, from Alejandra Pizarnik, *Diarios*, new edition edited by Ana Becciú (Madrid: Random House Mondadori, 2013), p. 278. Some of the earliest traces of French in Pizarnik's diary date from the end of September, 1954, recording subjects of study (she studied French at the Alliance Française during 1954 and 1955), including a quote from *Albertine Disparue* (*Albertine Gone*), the sixth volume of Marcel Proust's *À la recherché du temps perdu*: "[M]on plaisir ne serait plus dans le monde mais dans la littérature." ("My pleasure would no longer be in the world but in literature.") Pizarnik kept a writer's diary from 1950 to 1972, the year she died of an overdose.

3. All members from both sides of the family remaining in Równe (then part of the administrative region of Poland between 1918 and 1939) were killed. Before World War II and during the German occupation (1941–44), the city was located in Poland. It remained part of Soviet Ukraine until the breakup of the Soviet Union in 1991, the year the Ukrainian parliament officially adopted the name Rivne. Pizarnik's parents never returned to their homeland.

4. Paris appears as a destination in Pizarnik's diaries as early as July 24, 1955, curiously the same day she notes "no estudio francés, ya no voy a la Alliance [Française]." ("I don't study French, I no longer attend the Alliance Française.")

5. "In the Buenos Aires of the 1920s and 1930s, French influence was felt in painting, especially in the work of the first group of avant-garde painters known as *el grupo de París* . . . ; [the] Surrealist forerunner was undoubtedly Xul Solar of Argentina, and one of its first representatives was incontestably Antonio Berni" (Denis Rolland, "Paris and Latin Americans, Nineteenth and Twentieth Centuries. From Cultural Metropolis to Cultural

Museum?" in *Literary Cultures of Latin America, A Comparative History, Vol. II*, eds. Mario J. Valdés and Djelal Kadir [Oxford: Oxford University Press, 2004], p. 710.) Aldo Pellegrini, the father of Argentinian surrealism, established a few literary journals in Buenos Aires. Another name associated with surrealism in Argentina is Oliverio Girondo. Pizarnik was friends with both.

6. Pizarnik collected quotations and clippings in various notebooks. They were part of what she called the *palais du vocabulaire* [vocabulary palace], a compilation which she selected and incorporated into her own writings. In a green notebook dated "Mayo 1962 | Paris," we find Dickinson, Cummings, Pessoa, Valéry, Jarry, Senghor, G. Nouveau, Novalis, L. Milosz, Cavafy, Artaud, Reverdy, Pavese, Éluard, Cendrars, Mallarmé, Hölderlin, and Labbé, among others.

7. Ivonne Bordelois, *Correspondencia Pizarnik* (Buenos Aires: Seix Barral, 1998), p. 15.

8. From the outset, Pizarnik's "self-translations" weren't intended to follow the original. While some simply resemble the original, others show Pizarnik at work – in what may be considered transcreations.

9. The drawings are at the end of a notebook Pizarnik began in Paris, in November 1960, done with the same green marker as the inscription "Alejandra Pizarnik | Noviembre de 1960," which figures on the first page of the diary. In 1965 Pizarnik exhibited other drawings alongside those of her friend Manuel Mujica Láinez, the Argentine novelist, essayist, and art critic. The exhibition took place in Buenos Aires at the gallery "El Taller." Unpublished passages of Pizarnik's diaries contain small drawings (usually faces and human figures) interspersed throughout.

10. Princeton University acquired the bulk of Pizarnik's papers between 2002 and 2004. The first and largest part came from the Paris apartment of Aurora Bernárdez, widow of Julio Cortázar.

1.

POÈMES FRANÇAIS | FRENCH POEMS

Et quoi penser du silence? – Dormir oui, travailler quelques jours avec le rêve et m'épargner le silence. Il faut renverser tant de choses dans si peu de jours, faire un voyage si long dans si peu de jours. On me dit: choisis le silence ou le rêve. Mais je suis d'accord avec mes yeux ouverts qui devront aller – aller et ne jamais revenir – à cette zone de lumière vorace qui te mangera les yeux. Tu veux aller. Il le faut. Petit voyage fantôme. Quelques jours de travaux forcés pour ton regard. Ce sera comme toujours. Cette même douleur, cette désaffection. Ce non-amour. On meurt de sommeil ici. On aimerait se donner le plus vite possible. Quelqu'un a inventé ce plan sinistre: un retour au regard ancien, un aller à la recherche d'une attente faite des deux yeux bleues dans la poussière noire. Le silence est tentation et promesse. Le but de mon initiation. Le commencement de toute fin. C'est de moi que je parle. Il arrive qu'il faut aller une seule fois pour voir si pour une seule fois encore te sera donné de voir. On meurt de sommeil. On désire de ne pas bouger. On est fatiguée. Chaque os et chaque membre se rappelle ses anciens malheurs. On est souffrante et on rampe, on danse, on se traîne. Quelqu'un a promis. C'est de moi que je parle. Quelqu'un ne peut plus.

And what to think of silence? – To sleep yes, and to work a few days with the dream, sparing myself silence. Must reverse the course of so many things in such scant time, take this long trip in such scant time. They tell me: choose the silence or the dream. But I agree with my wide-open eyes going toward – going toward, never vacillating from – this zone of voracious light that will devour your eyes. You want to go, you must go. Little phantom trip. A few days of constrained draw on your gaze. It'll be as always. Same pain, this disaffection, this non-love. We die of fatigue here. We'd love to offer ourselves as quickly as possible. Someone has invented this sinister plan: a return to the archaic gaze, a going toward the expectation figured by two blue eyes in the black dust. Silence is temptation and promise. Finale of my initiation. Beginning of every end. It's of myself I speak. It happens to be necessary to go only once to see if just once again you'll be granted the vision. We die of fatigue here. We'd rather not move. We're exhausted. Each bone and each limb recalls its archaic sufferings. We suffer and crawl, dance, we drag ourselves. Someone has promised. It's of myself I speak. Someone can't take it anymore.

Si pour une fois de nouveau le regard bleu dans le sac rempli de poussière – je parle de moi, j'ai le droit – cette attente, cette patience – si pour une fois de nouveau – qui me comprend? – je parle des jouets brisés, je parle d'un sac noir, je parle d'une attente, je parle de moi, je peux le faire, je dois le faire. Si tout ce que j'appelle ne vient pas une seule fois encore quelqu'un devra rire, quelqu'un devra fêter une blague atroce – je parle de la lumière sale qui courre à travers la poussière, les yeux bleus qui patientent. Qui me comprend? Une seule fois encore la petite main entre les jouets brisés, le regard de celle qui attend, écoute, comprend. Les yeux bleus comme une réponse à cette mort qui est à côté de moi, qui me parle et c'est moi. Si pour une fois de nouveau mes yeux terrestres, ma tête enfoncée dans un sac noir, mes yeux bleus qui savent lire ce qui exprime la poussière, sa lamentable écriture. Si pour une fois encore.

If for once again the blue gaze inside this sack full of dust – I speak of myself, I have the right – this expectation, this patience – if for once again – who understands me? – I speak of broken toys, of a black sack, of an expectation, I speak of myself, I can do it, I ought to do it. If everything I call doesn't come to me just once again, someone will have to laugh, someone will have to toast with an atrocious joke – I speak of dust riven with sullen light, blue eyes patiently marking time. Who understands me? Just once again the small hand among broken toys, regard of her who waits, listens, understands. Blue eyes as a response to this death right next to me, which speaks to me and is me. If for once again my earthen eyes, my head stuffed in a black sack, my blue eyes which can read what dust scrawls, its pathetic handwriting. If again each time.

Tout le long du jour j'entends le bruit de l'eau pleurant. Ma mémoire, mon lieu sanglant, mon ancien ange mordu par le vent. Tout le jour je dors en pleurant pendant que les mots tombent comme l'eau déchirée, je tombe en pleurant, je me souviens du bruit de l'eau qui tombe dans mon rêve de toi. Toute la nuit j'écoute les pas de quelque chose qui vient à moi. Toute la nuit je dessine dans mes yeux la forme de tes yeux. Toute la nuit je nage dans tes eaux, je me noie dans mes yeux qui maintenant sont tes yeux. Toute la nuit je parle avec ta voix et je me dis ce que tu silences. Toute la nuit tu pleuves sur moi, pluie de mains d'eau qui me noient. Toute la nuit et tout le long du jour je regarde des tâches bleues dans un mur, à toute heure j'attends que le mot obscène serve à former ton visage. Je n'abandonne pas ce lieu de reconnaissance, je m'en vais seulement quand tu arrives.

Et tout le long du jour je dors en pleurant. Je me souviens du vent, toute la nuit je pense au vent qui vient à moi et reste en moi. Ma mémoire, un oiseau affolé sur la plage grise sous le vent froid qui vient et revient et ne s'en va pas. Le vent est en moi, tu es en moi, toute la nuit je pleure en me souvenant de l'eau qui tombe et de la rive froide sous le vent gris. Où est ton ancien savoir? – on me demande. Où est ton silence? Toute la nuit j'entends le bruit de mon visage qui pleure. Et c'est le chemin vers ton lieu natal, vers ta souffrance pure. Toute la nuit sous la pluie inconnue. À moi on m'a donnée un silence plein de formes – tu dis. Et tu cours désolée comme l'unique oiseau dans le vent.

All day long I hear the noise of moaning water. My memory, my bloody place, my archaic angel bitten by the wind. All day I sleep moaning while words fall like shredded water, I fall moaning, I remember the water's noise falling through my dream of you. All night I listen to the steps of something coming for me. All night I delineate in my eyes the form of your eyes. All night I'm swimming your waters, drowning in my eyes become your eyes. All night I speak with your voice and tell myself what you silence. All night you rain over me, rain of water-hands that drown me. All night and all day long I contemplate the blue stains on a wall, each passing hour pining for the obscene word that will form your face. I don't abandon this place of recognition, only relinquish it when you arrive.

And all day long I sleep moaning. I remember the wind, all night I think of the wind that comes to me and abides in me. My memory, a frenetic bird on the gray beach under the cold wind that comes and comes on again and won't leave. The wind in me, you in me, all night I cry remembering the water falling and the cold shore under the gray wind. Where is your archaic knowledge? – they ask me. Where is your silence? All night I hear the noise of my weeping face. And it's the course to your natal place, to your pure suffering. All night under the unknown rain. To me they've offered one silence full of forms – you say. And you go off desolate as the sole bird in the wind.

Toute la nuit j'entends le bruit de l'eau en pleurant. Toute la nuit je fais la nuit en moi, je fais le jour qui commence à cause de moi qui pleure parce que le jour tombe comme l'eau dans la nuit.

Toute la nuit j'entends la voix de quelqu'un qui me cherche. Toute la nuit tu m'abandonnes lentement comme l'eau qui pleure en tombant lentement. Toute la nuit j'écris des messages lumineux, des messages de pluie, toute la nuit quelqu'un me cherche et je cherche quelqu'un.

Le bruit des pas dans le cercle proche de lumière colérique qui naît de mon insomnie. Des pas de quelqu'un qui ne crie plus, n'écrit plus. Toute la nuit quelqu'un se retient et parcourt le cercle de lumière amère.

Toute la nuit je me noie dans tes yeux qui sont mes yeux. Toute la nuit je m'affole en cherchant l'habitant du cercle de mon silence. Toute la nuit je vois quelque chose pousser jusqu'à mon regard, quelque chose d'une matière silencieuse et humide et qui fait un bruit de quelqu'un qui pleure.

L'absence souffle grisement et la nuit est dense. La nuit a la couleur des paupières du mort, la nuit visqueuse, exhalant une huile noire qui m'affole et me fait chercher un lieu vide sans chaleur et sans froid. Toute la nuit je fuis quelqu'un. Je mène la poursuite et la fugue. Je chante un chant de deuil. Oiseaux noirs sur drapeaux noirs. Je crie mentalement. Le vent dément. Je m'en vais de la main tendue et crispée, je ne veux pas savoir autre chose que ce gémissement perpétuel, que ce bruit dans la nuit, cette lenteur, cette infamie, cette poursuite, cette inexistence.

Toute la nuit je sais que l'abandon c'est moi. Que la seule voix pleurant c'est moi. On peut chercher avec des falots, on peut parcourir le mensonge d'une ombre. On peut sentir que le cœur est dans la jambe et l'eau dans l'ancien lieu du cœur.

Toute la nuit je te demande pourquoi. Toute la nuit tu me dis *no*.

All night I hear the noise of water sobbing. All night I make night in me, I make the day that begins on my account, that sobs because day falls like water through night.

All night I hear the voice of someone seeking me out. All night you abandon me slowly like the water that sobs slowly falling. All night I write luminous messages, messages of rain, all night someone checks for me and I check for someone.

The noise of steps in the circle near this choleric light birthed from my insomnia. Steps of someone who no longer writhes, who no longer writes. All night someone holds back, then crosses the circle of bitter light.

All night I drown in your eyes become my eyes. All night I prod myself on toward that squatter in the circle of my silence. All night I see something lurch toward my looking, something humid, contrived of silence launching the sound of someone sobbing.

Absence blows grayly and night goes dense. Night, the shade of the eyelids of the dead, viscous night, exhaling some black oil that blows me forward and prompts me to search out an empty space without warmth, without cold. All night I flee from someone. I lead the chase, I lead the fugue. I sing a song of mourning. Black birds over black shrouds. My brain cries. Demented wind. I leave the tense and strained hand, I don't want to know anything but this perpetual wailing, this clatter in the night, this delay, this infamy, this pursuit, this inexistence.

All night I see that abandonment is me, that the sole sobbing voice is me. We can search with lanterns, cross the shadow's lie. We can feel the heart thud in the thigh and water subside in the archaic site of the heart.

All night I ask you why. All night you tell me *no*.

Une fois de nouveau, quelqu'un tombe dans sa première chute – chute des deux corps, des deux yeux, de quatre yeux verts ou de huit yeux verts si on compte aussi ceux qui naissent dans le miroir (à minuit, dans la peur la plus pure, dans la perte), tu n'a pas su reconnaître la voix de ton morne silence, tu n'a pas su voir les messages terrestres qui se dessinent au milieu d'un état fou, quand le corps est un verre et on boit de soi et de l'autre une sorte d'eau impossible.

Inutilement le désir verse sur moi une liqueur maudite. Pour ma soif assoiffée, qu'est-ce que peut la promesse d'un regard? Je parle de quelque chose qui n'est pas dans ce monde. Je parle de quelqu'un qui a son but ailleurs.

Et j'étais nue dans le souvenir de la nuit blanche. J'étais ivre et j'ai fait l'amour toute la nuit, exactement comme une chienne malade.

Parfois on subit trop de réalité dans l'espace d'une seule nuit. On se déshabille, on a trop d'horreur. On sait que le miroir sonne comme une montre, le miroir d'où jaillira le cri, ta déchirure.

La nuit s'ouvre une seule fois. Ça suffit. Tu vois. Tu as vu. La peur d'être deux dans le miroir, et tout de suite on est quatre. On crie, on gémit, ma peur, ma joie plus horrible que ma peur, mes paroles obscènes, mes paroles sont des clefs pour m'enfermer dans un miroir, avec toi, mais toujours seule. Et je sais bien de quoi est faite la nuit. On est tombée si profond dans une mâchoire qui ne s'attendait pas à ce sacrifice, à cette condamnation pour mes yeux qui ont vu. Je parle d'une découverte: avoir senti le moi dans le sexe, le sexe dans le moi. Je parle de laisser tomber la peur de chaque jour pour acquérir la peur d'un instant. Perte la plus pure. Mais qui me dira: ne pleure plus dans la nuit? Parce qu'aussi la folie est un mensonge. Comme la nuit. Comme la mort.

Once again, someone falls in their first falling – fall of the two bodies, of the two eyes, of four green eyes or eight green eyes if we count those born in the mirror (at midnight, in the purest fear, in loss), you haven't been able to recognize the voice of your dull silence, to behold the earthly messages scrawled in the middle of one mad state, when the body is a glass and from ourselves and from the other we drink some sort of impossible water.

Desire needlessly spills on me a cursed liqueur. For my thirsting thirst, what can the promise of contact with your eyes do? I speak of something not in this world. I speak of someone whose purpose is elsewhere.

And I was naked in memory of the white night. Drunk, and I made love all night, just like a sick dog.

Sometimes we suffer too much reality in the space of a single night. We get undressed, we're horrified. We're aware the mirror sounds like a watch, the mirror from which your cry will pour out, your laceration.

Night opens itself only once. It's enough. You see. You've seen. Fear of being two in the mirror, and suddenly we're four. We cry, we sob, my fear, my joy more horrible than my fear, my obscene words, my words which are keys locking me into a mirror, with you, but ever alone. I know the nature of night. We've fallen so completely into jaws which couldn't fathom this sacrifice, this condemnation of my seeing eyes. I speak of a discovery: felt the I in sex, sex in the I. I speak of burying everyday fear to secure the fear of an instant. The abyss of absence. But who'll say: don't cry at night? Because madness is a lie too. Like night. Like death.

alexandra et arta s'amusent pour jeannine à paris le deux septembre de l'an mil neuf cent soixante trois.

animal interdit
rentre avec la pluie
quand le jour nous dérange
et déplace l'ennui

ange offert sous les voûtes
ramasse nos chagrins
quand la nuit est un peu plus
que quelques petits soleils séparés
quand le cœur lâche un cri
qui sèche nos alarmes

gare aux anges mon amour
gare aussi aux discours
qui trainent sur nos lèvres
de poupées de bois de Jamaïque

"mais le jour pleut sur le vide de tout"

il existe encore des grimaces
si joliment parées que trop nombreux
sont ceux qui les volent en rires

Ris de l'obscurité des eaux

la nuit s'ouvre
je rentre
la nuit se ferme
je ne sors pas

alexandra and arta enjoy themselves for jeannine in paris on september second of the year nineteen hundred and sixty three.

forbidden animal
return with the rain
when the day deranges us
displacing our ennui

angel presented under the vaults
gather our grief
when the night is a bit more
than some little suns pulled apart
when the heart lets loose a cry
our disquietude wrings dry

mind the angels my love
mind also those words
dragging across our lips
lips of wooden Jamaican dolls

"but the day rains over the emptiness of everything"

there are still grimaces
so sweetly decked out that many
pilfer them for laughs

Laugh at the obscurity of waters

night opens
I enter
night shuts
I don't leave

ris de toi
ris de moi

il avance des heures qui mordent à nos joies.

laugh at yourself
laugh at myself

hours hours and hours snap up our pleasures.

Paroles du vent, un cheval rouge traverse la mémoire d'anciennes nuits de cris. Le mal naît dans mes yeux qui se rappellent. Le monde a la forme d'un cri. J'aurai aimé me voir dans une autre nuit, hors du délire d'être deux chemins du miroir. Façon de voir, les yeux ouverts cherchent la dernière trace. Un cheval rouge amène des saisons colériques. On mord le bout de son nom, on se perd dans le souvenir d'un cri. Si tout est comme ça, où sont les rois du non-savoir? Je me tends sur le temps d'un galop, des cris me traînent, la captive d'une seule trace, j'entends le bruit de ce qui détruit le vent. Cheval de la colère, amenez-moi loin de moi. Loin de ce cri qui est à la place de la nuit.

Words of the wind, a red horse careens across the memory of ancient wailing nights. Evil emerges from my memorious eyes. The world given form as a cry. How I would have loved to see myself some other night, beyond this madness of being both sides of the mirror. Means of seeing, the opened eyes glimpse the dissolving trace. A red horse foretells choleric seasons. Chewing the end of its name, we lose ourselves in the memory of a howl. If everything is like that, where are the kings of unknowing? I bend myself around the galloping hour, the hour of cries that drag me after them, captive to a single trace, I hear the sound of what beats down the wind. Horse of ire, bear me far from myself. Far from this cry that stands in for night.

Nue. Sommeil du corps transparent comme un arbre de verre. Tu entends près de toi la rumeur brutale d'un désir inextricable. Nuit aveuglément mienne. Tu es plus loin que moi. Horreur de te chercher dans l'espace rempli de cris de mon poème. Ton nom c'est la maladie des choses à minuit. On m'avait promis un silence. Ton visage est plus près de moi que le mien. Mémoire fantôme. Comme j'aimerais te tuer –

Naked. Fatigue of the body transparent as a glass-tree. Near yourself you hear the brutal rumor of inextricable desire. Night blindly mine. You're farther gone than me. Horror of checking for you in the screams of my poem. Your name is the disease of things at midnight. They had promised me one silence. Your face is closer to me than my own. Phantom memory. How I'd love to kill you –

à toi
le toit
à moi
les mois
mémoire
armoire de gloire
sale salle de sel
toi en haut
anneau annulé
les années les aînés
tout pèse
étrangle
étrange cercle
aime-moi
tu élis
je dis
personne dit
rien dit
le derrière du rideau
fait l'amour avec le vent
j'attends
qu'ils finissent
pour vivre
sans toi
à l'aube sans toi
je me vois nue
entre les déchets
qu'on rejette
chacun son lieu
de hurler
et de dire

to you
the view
to me
the months
memory
armoire of glory
sullen salon of salt
you up high
announcement annulled
the arc the archaic
everything's weight
strangles
strange circle
love me
it's your play
I say
no one says
nothing says
the back of the curtain
makes love to the wind
I wait
until they finish up
living
without you
at dawn without you
I see myself naked
among the dross
that we toss
each to her place
to cry
to speak

une absence
chacun son absence
j'ai choisi
je suis pure
j'ai bue pour le revoir
au fond du vin
ton cri en vain

an absence
to each her own absence
I’ve chosen
I’ve gone pure
I drank to see him again
at the bottom of your wine
your cry in vain

Je te cherche dans le vent. Tu n'es pas un cri. Mais je te cherche dans le vent.

La nuit m'ouvre et c'est toi.

Reviens encore une fois. Ton visage inexprimable m'a dit ce qu'est ma déchirure. Tes yeux aveuglent tout, même la nuit, ton nom écrit en moi.

Reviens comme toujours. Tes yeux sont mon seul mouvement vers l'autre face de la mort.

Chaque mot c'est toi qui le veux dire. Chaque mot est une longue initiation au souvenir.

Reviens, pendant que la nuit sonne et les miroirs s'ouvrent et tout se déchire dans son être à cause de ton absence. Tout veut avoir des rapports avec le vent, le ciel. Pour chercher un geste terrible, une manière d'être sans toi, un impossible.

Tes yeux commencent dans mes yeux qui ne te voient plus. Ils commencent dans ma voix qui ne te parle plus. Ils meurent dans mes mains qui ne te touchent plus. Tes yeux se dessinent sur ma peau. Je suis atroce à voir maintenant. Sinistre tatouage. Je fais la pluie et le soleil. À défaut de tes yeux dans mes yeux.

I check for you in the wind. You're not a cry. But I check for you in the wind.

Night opens me and it's you.

Return once again. Your inexpressible face revealed to me the inner tearing. Your eyes blind everything, even the night, your name written inside me.

Return as ever. Your eyes are my only conveyance to death's other face.

Each word is you begging to utter it. Each word is the long invitation to memory.

Return, while night clatters and mirrors open and everything tears inside because of your absence. Everything wants to get on with the wind, the sky. To register a terrible gesture, some way of being without you, an impossible.

Your eyes begin in my eyes which no longer see you. Begin in my voice which no longer speaks to you. Die out in my hands which no longer touch you. Your eyes are inscribed in my flesh. No one can bear to see me now. Sinister tattoo. I do the rain, I do the sun. For want of your eyes in my eyes.

Souvenir près de l'oubli. Mort lointaine
la voix grince et trépide et tremble
le vent dément
le vent ment
le vain vent
la main ment
la main sainte
le vent saint
le saint enceinte
par le vent qui ment
je mens
je m'en démens
je m'endors
d'or et d'ouïr
j'ai mes mains démentes
mes saintes mains
enceintes de ton ombre
je m'effondre
je m'effleure
un geste de fleur
frêle
froide
je m'offre affreusement
gouffre givre
je m'offre
tu m'effraies
je m'offre
je m'en fous

Memory near oblivion. Far death
the voice grinds and vibrates and trembles
the wind denies
the wind lies
the vain wind
the hand hides
the holy hand
the sent saint
the saint inseminated
by the wind that lies
I lie
I deny
I lie down
from gold and from grind
these demented hands are mine
my holy hands
inseminated by your shadow
I collapse
I touch myself
a flower's gesture
frail
cold
I offer myself awfully
abyss frost
I offer myself
you frighten me
I offer myself
I don't give a fuck

le temps tombant dans le vide de mes
yeux clos

voici l'ange colérique

la plume verte
la fenêtre ouverte

the hour sinking into the emptiness of my
closed eyes

here the choleric angel

the green feather
the open window

Votre amant vous a regardé

avec mes yeux qui sont dans ses yeux
et qui lui gardent jour et nuit

dans ses paupières je dors jusqu'à l'aube

dans ses yeux j'ai appris à connaître
sa dernière nudité

N'oublie pas tes yeux
parce que c'est là où j'habite

Your lover has taken you in

with my eyes which are in his eyes
and which keep watch day and night

in his eyelids I sleep until dawn

in his eyes I've come to know
a last nakedness

Don't forget your eyes
because I inhabit them

1

Et quoi penser du silence? – Dormir oui, travailler quelques jours avec
le rêve et m'épargner le silence. Il faut renverser tant de
choses dans si peu de jours, faire un voyage si long dans si
peu de jours. On me dit: choisis le silence ou le rêve. Mais
je suis d'accord avec mes yeux ouverts qui devront aller
– aller et jamais revenir – à cette zone de lumière vorace qui
te mangera les yeux. Tu veux aller. Il le faut. Petite voyage
fantôme. Quelques jours des travaux forcés pour ton regard.
Ce sera comme toujours. Cette même douleur, cette désaffection.
Cet non-amour. On meurt de sommeil ici. On aimerait se
donner le plus vite possible. Quelqu'un a inventé ce plan
sinistre: un retour au [illegible] regard ancien, un aller
à la recherche d'une attente faite des deux yeux bleus
dans la poussière noire. Le silence est tentation et promesse.
Le but de mon initiation. Le commencement de toute fin.
C'est de moi que je parle. Il arrive qu'il faut aller
une seule fois pour voir si pour une seule fois
encore te sera donné de voir. On meurt de sommeil.
On désire de ne pas bouger. On est fatiguée. Chaque os
et chaque membre se rappelle ses anciens malheurs.
On est souffrante et on rampe, on danse, on se traîne.
Quelqu'un a promis. C'est de moi que je parle.
Quelqu'un ne peut plus.

Et quoi penser du silence? | *And what to think of silence?* (p. 19)

si pour une fois de nouveau le regard bleu dans le sac rempli de poussière [illegible]
[illegible] - je parle de moi, j'ai le droit - cette attente, cette patience - si pour
une fois de nouveau - qui me comprend? - je parle des jouets brisés,
je parle d'un sac noir, je parle d'une attente, je parle de moi, je
le peux faire, je le dois faire. Si tout ce que j'appelle ne vient pas une
seul fois encore quelqu'un devra rire, quelqu'un devra fêter
une blague atroce - je parle de la lumière sale qui coure à travers
la poussière, les yeux bleues qui patientent. Qui me comprend?
Une seule fois encore la petite main [illegible] entre les
jouets brisés, le regard de celle qui attend, ecoutte, comprend.
Les yeux bleues comme une réponse à cette mort qui est
à côté de moi, qui me parle et c'est moi. Si pour une
fois de nouveau mes yeux tervcentres, ma tête enfoncée
dans un sac noire, mes yeux bleues qui savent lire
ce qui exprime la poussière, sa lamentable écriture.
Si pour une fois encore.

Si pour une fois de nouveau | *If for once again* (p. 21)

3

Tout le long du jour j'entends le bruit de l'eau pleurant. Ma mémoire, mon lieu sanglant, mon ancien ange mordu par le vent. Tout le jour je dorme en pleurant pendant que les mots tombent comme l'eau delivrée, je tombe en pleurant, je me souviens du bruit de l'eau qui tombe dans mon rêve de toi. Toute la nuite j'écoute les pas de quelque chose qui vient à moi. Toute la nuite je dessine dans mes yeux la forme ~~[illegible]~~ de tes yeux. Toute la nuit je nage dans tes eaux, je me ~~perds~~ noie dans mes yeux qui maintenant sont tes yeux. Toute la nuit je parle avec ta voix et je me dis ce que tu silences. Toute la nuite tu pleuves sur moi, pluie de mains d'eau qui me noient. Toute la nuit et tout le long du jour je regard des taches bleues dans un mur, à toute heure j'attende que le mot obscène serte à former ton visage. Je n'abandonne pas ce lieu de reconnaissance, je m'en vais seulement quand tu arrives.

Et tout le long du jour je dorme en pleurant. Je me souvient du vent, toute la nuite je pense au vent qui vient à moi et reste en moi. Ma mémoire, un oiseau affolé sur la plage grise sous le vent froid qui vient et revient et ne s'en va pas. Le vent est en moi, tu est en moi, toute la nuit je pleure en me souvenant de l'eau qui tombe et de la rive froid sous le vent gris. Où est ton ancien savoir? - on me demande. Où est ton silence? Tout la nuit j'entend le bruit de mon visage qui pleure. Et c'est le chemin vers ton lieu natal, vers ta souffrance pure. Toute la ~~no~~ nuite sous la pluie inconnue. À moi on m'a donnée un silence plein des formes - tu dis. Et tu cours désolée comme l'unique oiseau dans le vent.

Tout le long du jour | *All day long* (p. 23)

4

Toute la nuit j'entends le bruit de l'eau en pleurant. Toute la nuit je fais la nuit dans moi, je fais le jour qui commence à cause de moi qui pleure parce que le jour tombe comme l'eau dans la nuit. Toute la nuite j'entends la voix de quelqu'un qui me cherche. Toute la nuite tu m'abandonnes lentament ~~comme l'eau qui pleure en tombant~~ lentement. Toute la nuite j'écris des messages lumineuses, des messages de pluie, toute la nuite quelqu'un me cherche et je cherches à quelqu'un.

Le bruit des pas dans le cercle proche de lumière colérique qui naît de mon insomnie. Des pas de quelqu'un qui ne ne crit plus, n'écrit plus. Toute la nuite quelqu'un se retienne et parcourt le cercle de lumière amère.

Toute la nuit je me voie dans tes yeux qui ~~sont~~ mes yeux.

Toute la nuit je m'affole en cherchant l'habitant du cercle de mon silence. Toute la nuite je vois quelque chose pousser jusqu'à mon regard, quelque chose d'une matière silencieuse et humide et qui fait un bruit de quelqu'un qui pleure.

L'absence ~~souffle~~ grisement et la nuite est dense. La nuit à la couleur des paupières de mort, la nuit visqueuse, exhalant une huile noir qui m'affole et me fait chercher un lieu vide sans chaleur et sans froid. Toute la nuite je fuis de quelqu'un. Je mène la porsuite et la fugue. Je chante un chant de deuil. Oiseaux noirs sur drapeaux noirs. Je cris mentalment. Le vent dement. Je m'en vais de la main tendue et crispée, je ne veux pas savoir autre chose que ce gemissement perpetuel, que cet bruit dans la nuit, cette lenteur, cette infamie, cette porsuite, cette inexistence.

Toute la nuit je sais que l'abandon c'est moi. Que la seul voix pleurant c'est moi. On peut chercher avec des falots, on peut parcourir le mensonge d'une ombre. On peut sentir que le coeur est dans la jambe et l'eau dans l'ancien lieu du coeur.

Toute la nuit je te demandes pourquoi. Toute la nuit tu me dis no.

Toute la nuit | All night (p. 25)

5

Le sexe, la nuit.

Une fois de nouveau, quelqu'un tombe dans sa première chute -chute des deux corps, des deux yeux, de quatre yeux verts ou de huit yeux vertes si on compte aussi ceux qui naissent dans le miroir (à minuit, dans la peur la plus pure, dans la perte), tu n'as pas su reconnaître la voix de ton morne silence, tu n'a pas su voir les messages terrestres qui se dessinent au milieu d'un état fou, quand le corps est un verre et on boit de soi et de l'autre une sorte d'eau impossible.

Inutilement le désir verse sur moi une liqueur maudite. Pour ma soif assoiffée, qu'est-ce que peut la promesse d'un regard? Je parle de quelque chose qui n'est pas dans ce monde. Je parle de quelqu'un qui a son but ailleurs.

Et j'étais nue dans le souvenir de la nuit blanche. J'étais ivre et j'ai fait l'amour toute la nuit, exactement comme une chienne malade.

Parfois on reconnaît trop de realité dans l'espace d'une seule nuit. On se déshabille, on a trop d'horreur. On sait que le miroir sonne comme une montre, le miroir d'où jaillira le cri, ta déchirure.

La nuit s'ouvre une seule fois. Ça suffit. Tu vois. Tu as vu. La peur d'être deux dans le miroir, et tout de suite on est quatre. On crie, on gémit, ma peur, ma joie plus horrible que ma peur, mes paroles obscènes, mes paroles sont des clefs pour m'enfermer dans un miroir, avec toi, mais toujours seule. Et je sais bien de quoi est faite la nuit, on a tombée si profond dans une machoire qui ne s'attendait pas cet sacrifice, cette condamnation pour mes yeux qui ont vu. Je parle d'une découverte: avoir sentie le moi dans le sexe, le sexe dans le moi. Je parle de laisser tomber la peur de chaque jour pour acquérir la peur d'un instant. Perte la plus pure. Mais qui me dira: ne pleure plus dans la nuit? Parce que aussi la folie est un mensonge. Comme la nuit. Comme la mort.

Alejandra Pizarnik. décembre 1961

LE SEXE, LA NUIT | SEX, NIGHT (p. 27)

6

alexendra et arta s'amusent pour jeannine à paris le deux septembre de l'an mil neuf cent soixante trois.

animal interdit
rentre avec la pluie
quand le jour nous dérange
et déplace l'ennui

ange offert sous les voûtes
ramasse nos chagrins
quand la nuit est un peu plus
que quelques petits soleils séparés
quand le coeur lache un cri
q ui sèche nos alarmes

gare aux anges mon amour
gare aussi aux discours
qui trainent sur nos lèvres
de poupées de bois de Jamaique

"mais le jour pleut sur le vide de tout"

il existe encore des grimaces
si joliment parées que trop nombreux
sont ceux qui les volent en rires

Ris de l'obscurité des eaux

la nuit s'ouvre
je rentre
la nuit se ferme
je ne sors pas

ris de toi
ris de moi

il avance des heures qui mordent à nos joies.

alexandra et arta | *alexandra and arta* (p. 29)

Paroles du vent, un cheval rouge traverse
la mémoire d'anciens nuits de cris.
Le mal naît dans mes yeux
qui se rappellent. Le monde a la forme
d'un cri. J'aurais aimais me voir dans
une autre nuit, hors du délire d'être
deux chemin du miroir. Façon de
voir, les yeux ouverts cherchent la
dernière trace. Un cheval rouge
amène des saisons colériques. On
mord le bout de son nom, on
se perd dans le souvenir d'un
cri. Si tout est comme ça,
~~où sont les aveugles~~, où sont
les rois du non-savoir. Je
me tends sur le temps d'un
galop, des cris me traînent,
la captive d'une seule trace,
je entends le bruit de ce
qui détruit le vent. Cheval de
la colère, amenez-moi loin
de moi. Loin de ce cri qui
est à la place de la nuit.

Poemas franceses

Paroles du vent | *Words of the wind* (p. 33)

Nue. Sommeil du corps transparent comme
un arbre de verre. Tu entends près de toi
la rumeur brutale d'un désir inextricable.
Nuit aveuglément mienne. Tu est plus loin
que moi. Horreur de te chercher dans l'espace
rempli de cris de mon poème. Ton nom c'est
la maladie des choses à minuit. On m'avait
promit un silence. Ton visage est plus
près de moi que le mien. Mémoire fantôme.
On aimerais tuer.
Comme j'aimerai te tuer—

à toi
le toit [illegible]
à moi
les mois
~~l'oubli~~
~~fin~~
mémoire
~~gloire~~
armoire de gloire
sale salle de sel
toi en haut
~~[illegible]~~ anneau annulé
les années les aînés
tout ~~frère~~
~~[illegible]~~
étrangle
étrange cercle
~~de lumière fausse~~
~~[illegible]~~
aime-moi
tu dis
je dis

personne dit
rien dit
le derrière du rideau
fait l'amour avec le vent
j'attends
qu'il finissent
pour vivre
sans toi
à l'aube sans toi
~~[illegible] sans toi~~
je me vois nue
~~[illegible]~~
entre les déchets
qu'on rejette
chacun son lieu
de hurler
et de dire
une absence
chacun son absence
j'ai choisie
je suis pure
~~jusqu'à la nausée~~
j'ai bue pour le raisin
au fond du vin
ton cri en vain

Nue | *Naked* (p. 35)
à toi | *to you* (p. 37)

Je te cherche dans le vent | *I check for you in the wind* (p. 41)

Souvenir près de l'oubli. Mort lointain
La voix grince et trépide et tremble
le vent dément
le vent ment
le vain vent
la main ment
la main saint
le ~~saint~~ vent saint
le saint enceinte
par le vent qui ment
je mens
je ~~vous~~ m'en démens
je ~~[illegible]~~ m'en dors
d'or et ~~[illegible]~~ d'ivre
j'ai mes mains démentes
mes saints mains
enceintes de ton ombre
je m'effondre
je m'effleure
un geste de fleur
frêle
froide
je m'offre affreusement
gouffre givre
je m'offre
~~je~~ tu m'effrais
je m'offre
je m'en fous

Souvenir près de l'oubli | *Memory near oblivion* (p. 43)

le temps tombant dans le vide de mes
yeux clos

voici l'ange colérique

la plume verte
la fenetre ouverte

le temps tombant | *the hour sinking* (p. 45)

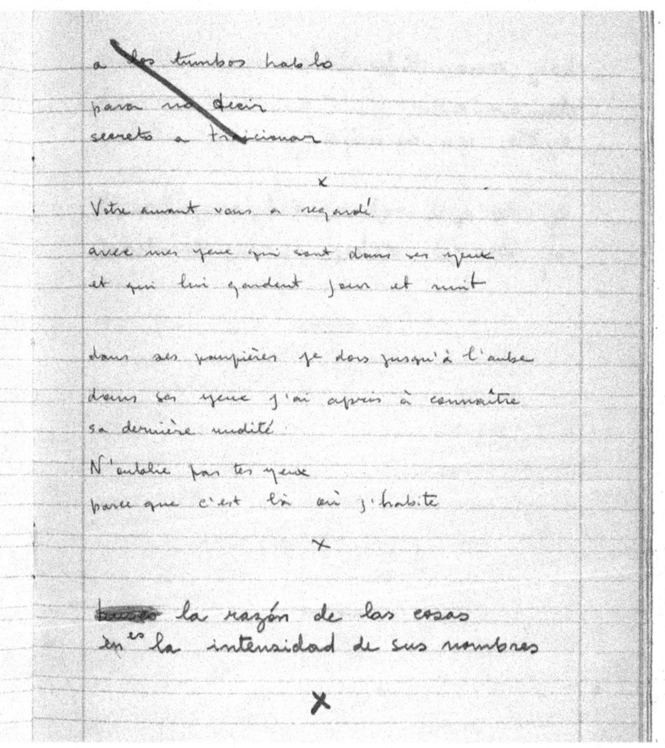

a los tumbos hablo
para no decir
secretos a traicionar

x

Votre amant vous a regardé
avec mes yeux qui sont dans ses yeux
et qui lui gardent jour et nuit

dans ses paupières je dors jusqu'à l'aube
dans ses yeux j'ai appris à connaître
sa dernière nudité
N'oublie pas tes yeux
parce que c'est là où j'habite

x

la razón de las cosas
en es la intensidad de sus nombres

x

Votre amant | *Your lover* (p. 47)

The page contains text in Spanish:

> a los tumbos hablo
> para no decir
> secreto a traicionar
> (stumbling around I speak
> to keep
> from betraying a secret)
>
> la razón de las cosas
> es la intensidad de sus nombres
> (the sense of things
> remains in the intensity of their names)

II.

AUTRES POÈMES FRANÇAIS | OTHER FRENCH POEMS

la nuit respirer la nuit
tu ne parles pas
tu ne te parles plus

même celle de la glace
a disparu

night breathing the night
you don't speak
you no longer speak to yourself

even the she in the mirror
has disappeared

la mort est ici
elle est ici
elle est derrière elle
derrière l'ombre de son ombre

quand arrivera-t-elle à elle?

death is here
she's here
she's behind her
behind the shadow of her shadow

when will she come to her?

un sommeil radieux
derrière la grille émerveillé
mourir de feu épanoui
avoir bu le sortilège de la pluie

a radiant sleep
behind the gate enraptured
to die of blooming fire
having consumed the curse of rain

Je joue un air d'amour aux cordes de cristal
De cette douce pluie où s'apaise mon mal

With crystal chords I play love's very tune
In soft falling rain that allays my wound

Et maintenant
que vais je faire
de tout ce temps
que sera ma vie
de tous ces gens
qui m'indiffèrent
maintenant,
que tu es partie
toutes ces nuits
pourquoi, pour qui
et ce matin
qui revient pour rien
ce cœur qui bat
pour qui pourquoi
qui bat très fort,
très fort,
et maintenant
que vais je faire
vers quel néant
glissera ma vie
ô mes amis
soyez gentils
vous savez bien
que l'on n'y peut rien
Et maintenant
que vais je faire
maintenant
que tu . . .

And now
what will I do
with all this time
that forms my life
with all these people
who care nothing for me
now,
that you've left
all these nights
why, for whom
and this morning
for nothing returning
my heart banging
for whom why
banging gravely,
gravely,
and now
how to face up to
that nothingness
my life slipping
o friends
be gentle
you know well
we have nothing to do with it
And now
what will I do
now
that you …

oh la lengua en el lugar
donde se viene a esta
tierra

ma langue
ou ma lampe
ma langue est la prêtresse

oh language already here
when we come to this
earth

my language
or my lamp
my language is the priestess

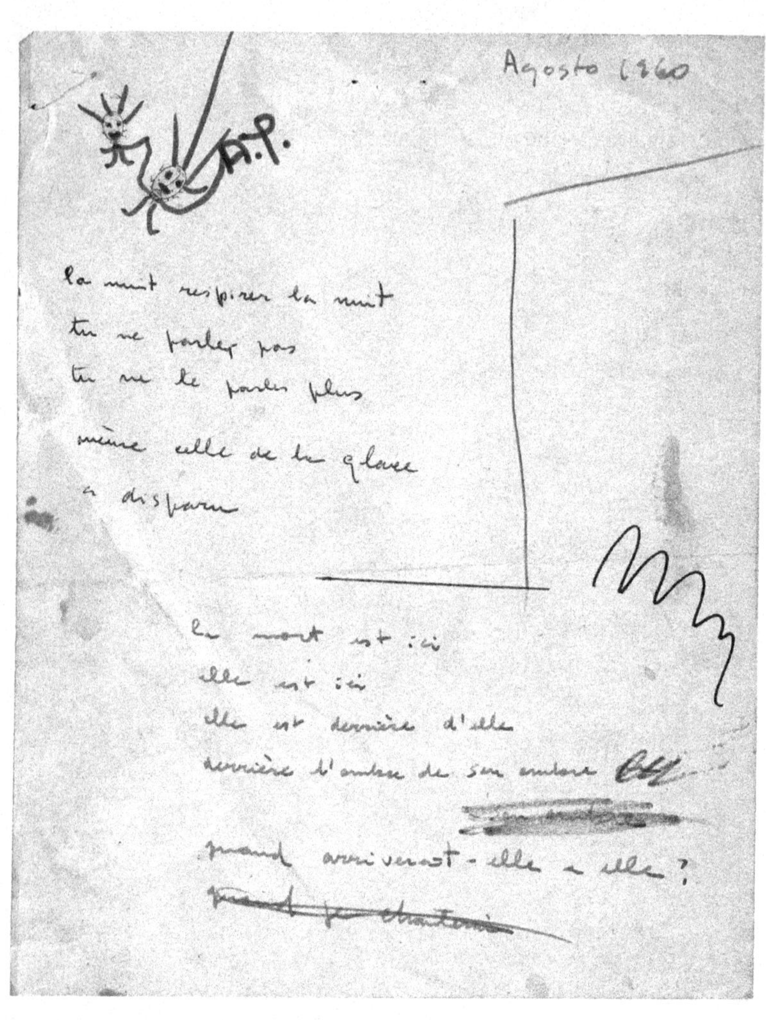

Agosto 1960

A.P.

la nuit respirer la nuit
tu ne parles pas
tu ne le parles plus

même celle de la glace
a disparu

la mort est ici
elle est ici
elle est derrière d'elle
derrière l'ombre de son ombre

quand arrivera-t-elle à elle?

la nuit respirer la nuit | *night breathing the night* (p. 63)
la mort est ici | *death is here* (p. 65)

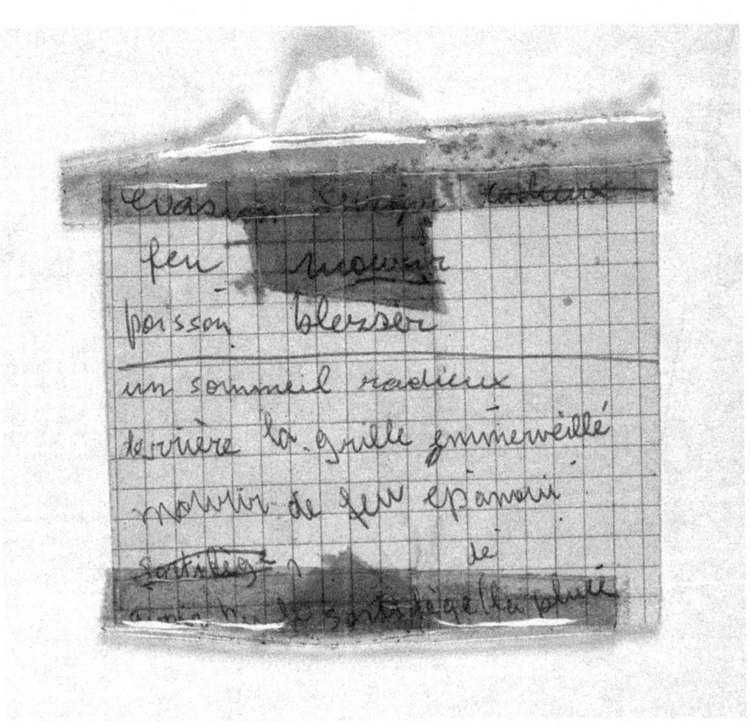

un sommeil radieux | *a radiant sleep* (p. 67)

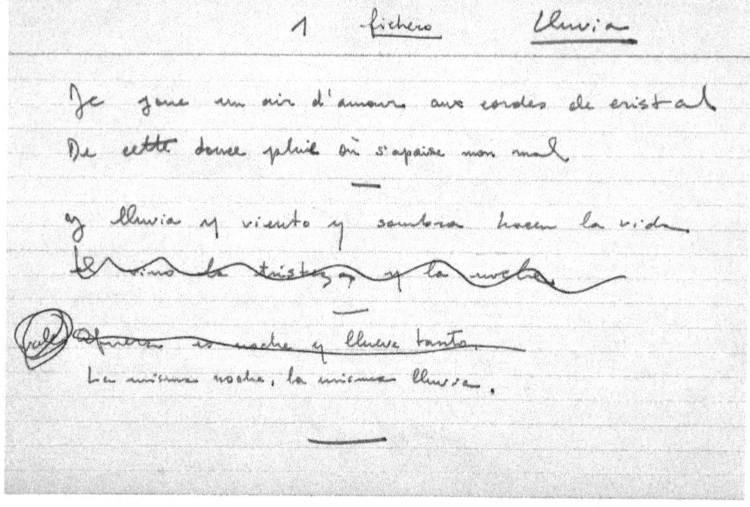

1 fichero lluvia

Je joue un air d'amour aux cordes de cristal
De cette douce pluie où s'apaise mon mal

y lluvia y viento y sombra hacen la vida
~~el vino la tristeza y la noche~~

~~Afuera es noche y llueve tanto.~~
La misma noche, la misma lluvia.

Je joue un air d'amour aux cordes de cristal |
With crystal chords I play love's very tune (p. 69)

The page also contains text in Spanish:

1 *fichero lluvia* | 1 *notecard rain*

y la lluvia y viento y sombra hacen la vida
el vino la tristeza y la noche

(and rain and wind and shadow make life)
(the wine the sadness and the night)

Afuera es noche y llueve tanto.
La misma noche, la misma lluvia.

(Outside is night and it rains much.)
(The same night, the same rain.)

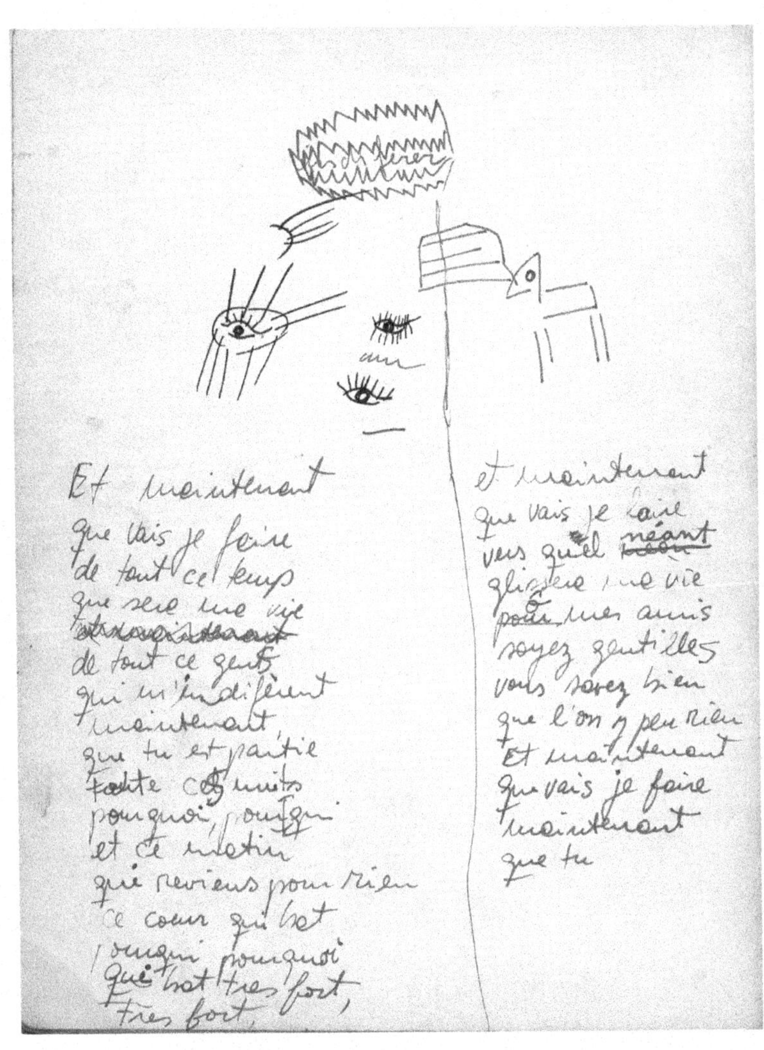

Et maintenant
que vais je faire
de tout ce temps
que sera ma vie
de tout ce gents
qui m'indifèrent
maintenant
que tu est partie
toute ces nuits
pourquoi, pourqui
et ce matin
qui reviens pour rien
ce coeur qui bat
pourqui pourquoi
qui bat très fort,
très fort,

et maintenant
que vais je faire
vers quel néant
glissera ma vie
mes amis
soyez gentilles
vous savez bien
que l'on y peu rien
Et maintenant
que vais je faire
maintenant
que tu

Et maintenant | *And now* (p. 71)

oh la lengua en el lugar
donde se viene a esta
tierra

ma langue
ou ma lampe
ma langue est la pretresse

oh la lengua en el lugar | oh language already here (p. 73)

ANNEXES

DESSINS | DRAWINGS

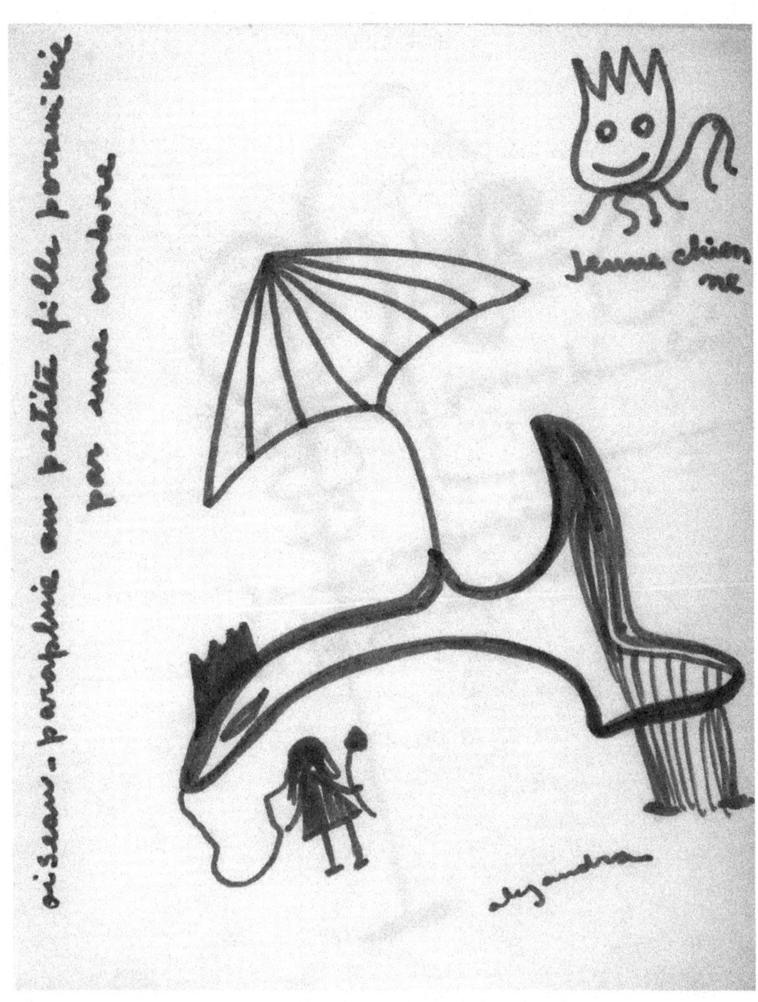

oiseau-parapluie ou petite fille poursuivie par une ombre
bird-umbrella or little girl hounded by a shadow

jeune chienne | young hussy

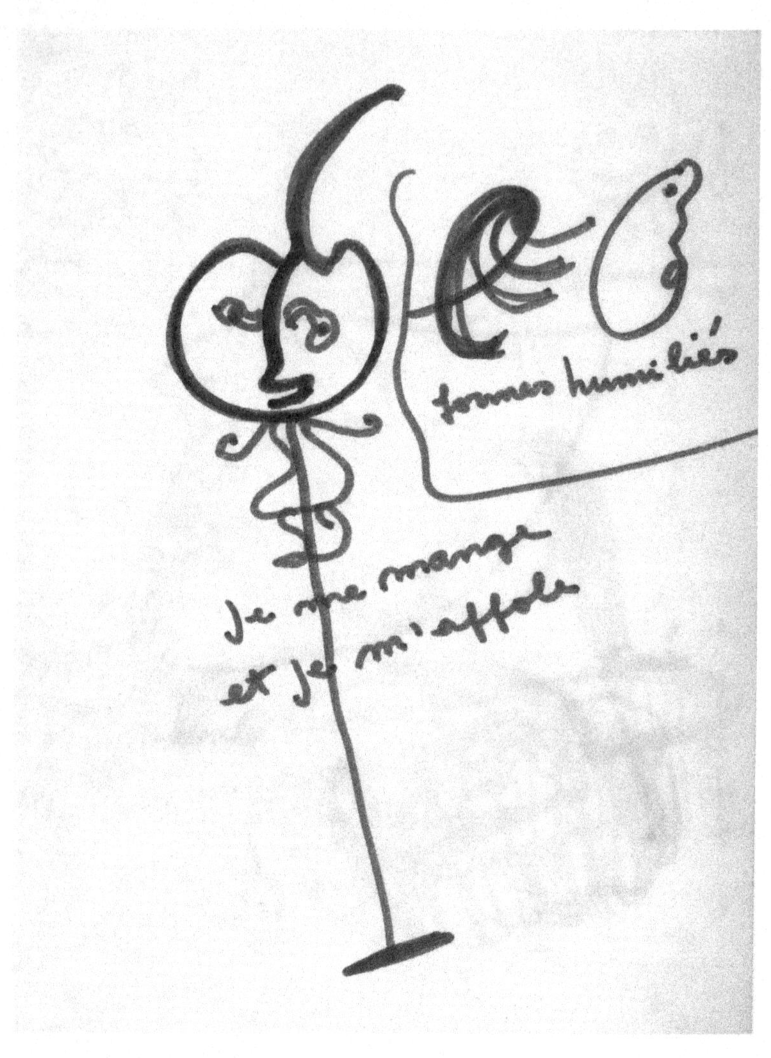

je me mange et je m'affole
devouring myself and panicking

formes humiliées | humiliated forms

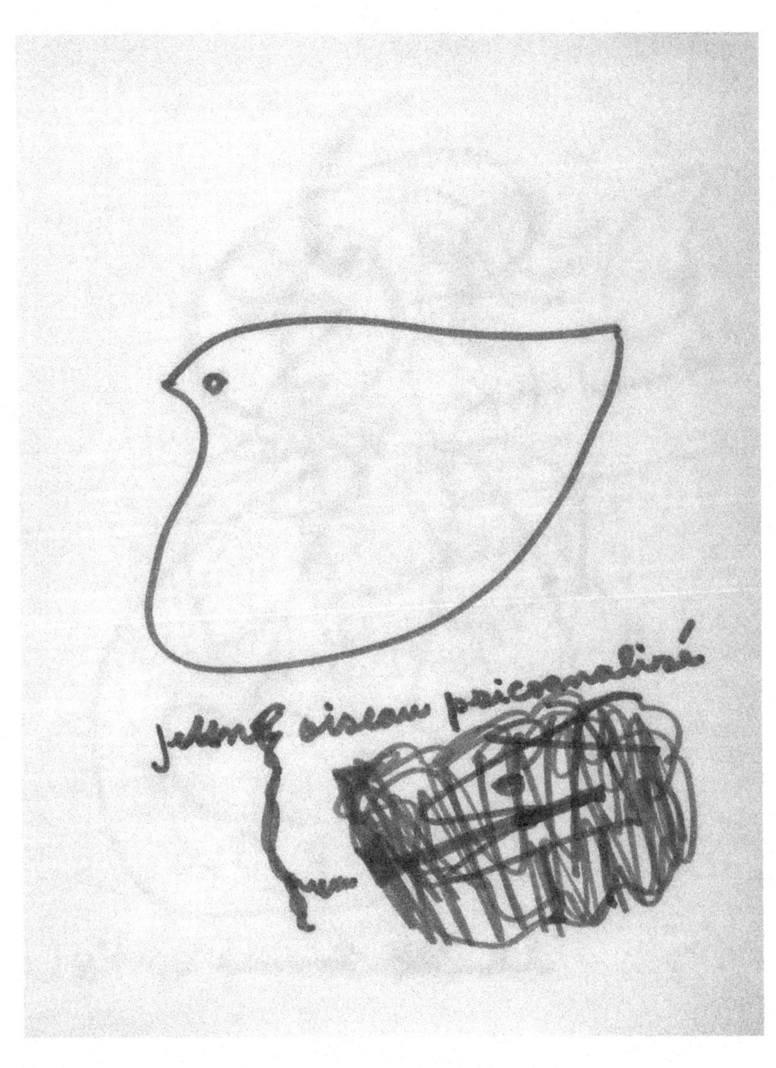

jeune oiseau psychanalysé | psychoanalyzed birdie

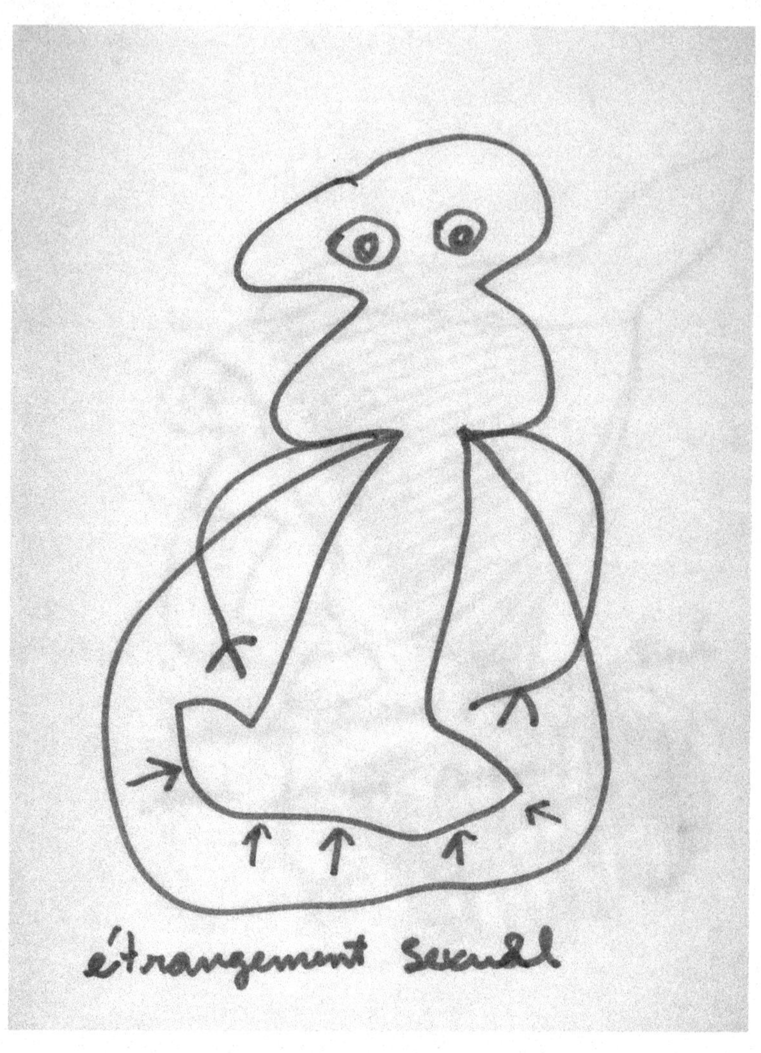

étrangement sexuel | strangely sexual

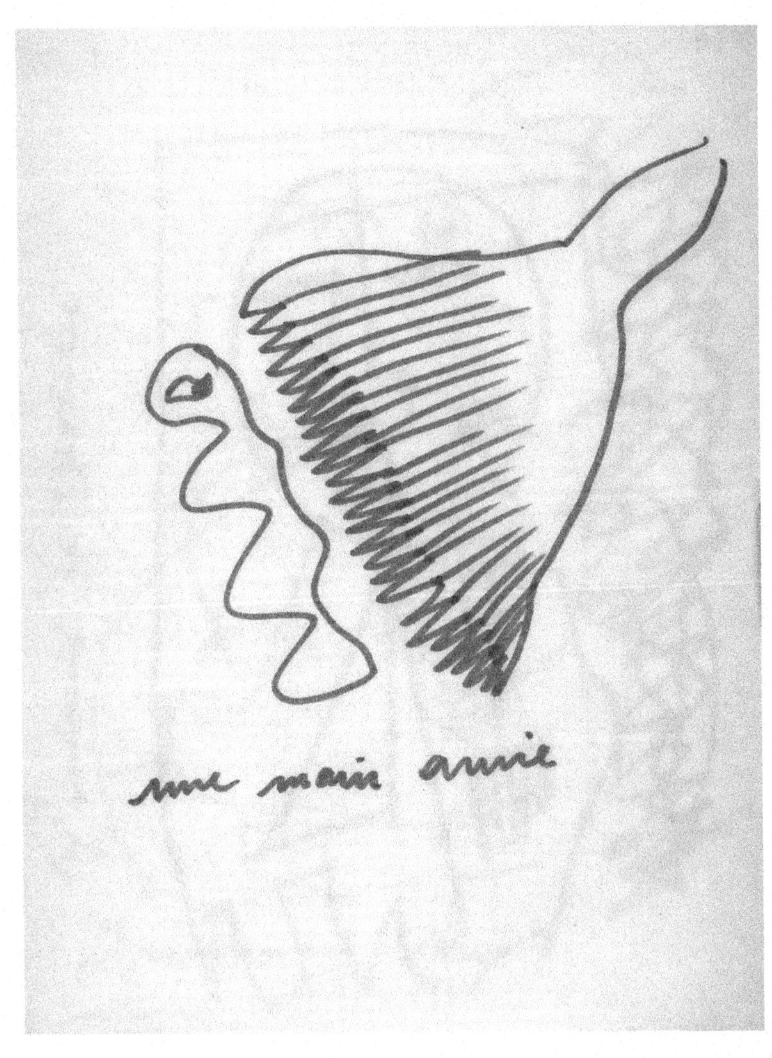

une main amie | a friendly hand

la volonté de tristesse | *the will to sadness*

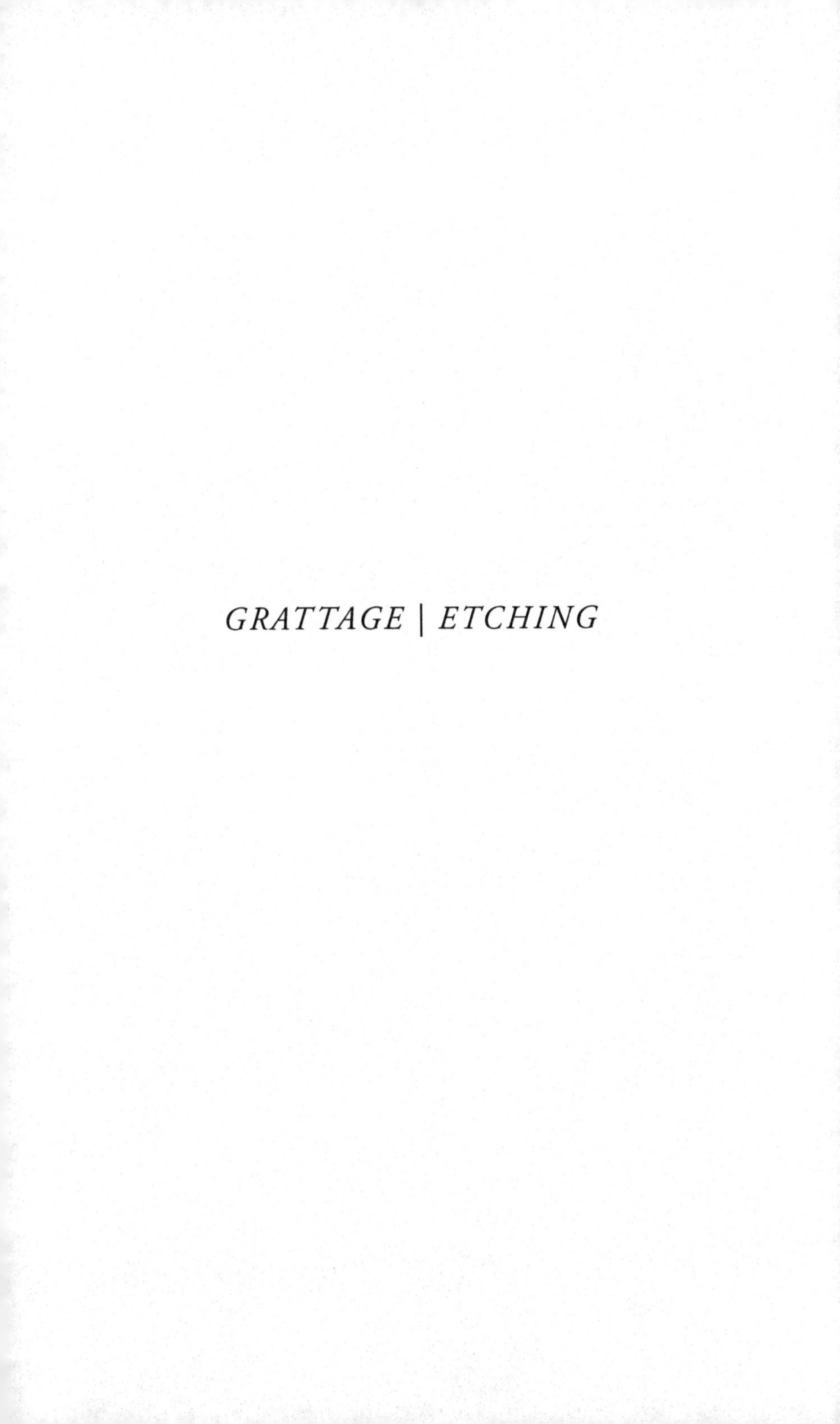

GRATTAGE | ETCHING

je me rappelle le vent, le lilas, le gris, le parfum, la chanson
et le vent, mais je ne me rappelle pas ce qu'a dit l'ange.

(I recall the wind, the lilacs, the gray, the perfume, the song,
and the wind, but I don't recall what the angel said.)

ACKNOWLEDGMENTS

THANKS TO

Barbara Epler and Declan Spring, publisher and senior editor at New Directions, for believing in this book and making it possible;

Erik Rieselbach, art director and production manager at New Directions, for his diligent work and suggestions at various stages;

Eileen Baumgartner, for her amazing design work;

Brittany Dennison, codirector of publicity at New Directions;

Ana Becciú, for supporting this project since our first discussion at the Gare de Lyon, Paris, on a winter afternoon in 2014;

Myriam Pizarnik de Nesis, for opening her private collection comprised mainly of books from Alejandra's private library;

Ivonne Bordelois, for putting at my disposal Pizarnik's unpublished *cahier vert* [green notebook], in which Pizarnik collected citations and poems by various authors;

Don C. Skemer and the rest of the personnel at Firestone Library, Princeton University, for their assistance during the four periods when I consulted the Alejandra Pizarnik Papers;

Cristina Piña for sharing biographical information and scholarship regarding Pizarnik's Paris years;

The Paris Review, where the poems "à toi" ("to you") and "Souvenir près de l'oubli" ("Memory near oblivion") appeared in the Spring issue.

New Directions Paperbooks—a partial listing

Kaouther Adimi, Our Riches
Adonis, Songs of Mihyar the Damascene
César Aira, Artforum
An Episode in the Life of a Landscape Painter
Ghosts
Will Alexander, The Sri Lankan Loxodrome
Osama Alomar, The Teeth of the Comb
Guillaume Apollinaire, Selected Writings
Paul Auster, The Red Notebook
White Spaces
Ingeborg Bachmann, Malina
Honoré de Balzac, Colonel Chabert
Djuna Barnes, Nightwood
Charles Baudelaire, The Flowers of Evil*
Bei Dao, City Gate, Open Up
Mei-Mei Berssenbrugge, Empathy
Max Blecher, Adventures in Immediate Irreality
Roberto Bolaño, By Night in Chile
Distant Star
Jorge Luis Borges, Labyrinths
Seven Nights
Coral Bracho, Firefly Under the Tongue*
Kamau Brathwaite, Ancestors
Basil Bunting, Complete Poems
Anne Carson, Glass, Irony & God
Norma Jeane Baker of Troy
Horacio Castellanos Moya, Senselessness
Camilo José Cela, Mazurka for Two Dead Men
Louis-Ferdinand Céline
Death on the Installment Plan
Journey to the End of the Night
Rafael Chirbes, On the Edge
Inger Christensen, alphabet
Julio Cortázar, All Fires the Fire
Cronopios & Famas
Jonathan Creasy, ed: Black Mountain Poems
Robert Creeley, If I Were Writing This
Guy Davenport, 7 Greeks
Osamu Dazai, No Longer Human
H.D., Selected Poems
Helen DeWitt, The Last Samurai
Some Trick
Marcia Douglas
The Marvellous Equations of the Dread
Daša Drndić, EEG
Robert Duncan, Selected Poems
Eça de Queirós, The Maias
William Empson, 7 Types of Ambiguity
Mathias Énard, Compass
Tell Them of Battles, Kings & Elephants
Shusaku Endo, Deep River
Jenny Erpenbeck, The End of Days
Go, Went, Gone
Lawrence Ferlinghetti
A Coney Island of the Mind
F. Scott Fitzgerald, The Crack-Up
On Booze
Jean Frémon, Now, Now, Louison
Rivka Galchen, Little Labors
Forrest Gander, Be With
Romain Gary, The Kites
Natalia Ginzburg, The Dry Heart
Happiness, as Such
Henry Green, Concluding
Felisberto Hernández, Piano Stories
Hermann Hesse, Siddhartha
Takashi Hiraide, The Guest Cat
Yoel Hoffmann, Moods
Susan Howe, My Emily Dickinson
Debths
Bohumil Hrabal, I Served the King of England
Qurratulain Hyder, River of Fire
Sonallah Ibrahim, That Smell
Rachel Ingalls, Binstead's Safari
Mrs. Caliban
Christopher Isherwood, The Berlin Stories
Fleur Jaeggy, Sweet Days of Discipline
Alfred Jarry, Ubu Roi
B.S. Johnson, House Mother Normal
James Joyce, Stephen Hero
Franz Kafka, Amerika: The Man Who Disappeared
Investigations of a Dog
Yasunari Kawabata, Dandelions
John Keene, Counternarratives
Heinrich von Kleist, Michael Kohlhaas
Alexander Kluge, Temple of the Scapegoat
Taeko Kono, Toddler-Hunting
Laszlo Krasznahorkai, Satantango
Seiobo There Below
Ryszard Krynicki, Magnetic Point
Eka Kurniawan, Beauty Is a Wound
Mme. de Lafayette, The Princess of Clèves
Lautréamont, Maldoror
Siegfried Lenz, The German Lesson
Denise Levertov, Selected Poems

Li Po, Selected Poems
Clarice Lispector, The Hour of the Star
The Passion According to G. H.
Federico García Lorca, Selected Poems*
Three Tragedies
Nathaniel Mackey, Splay Anthem
Xavier de Maistre, Voyage Around My Room
Stéphane Mallarmé, Selected Poetry and Prose*
Javier Marías, Your Face Tomorrow (3 volumes)
Bernadette Mayer, The Bernadette Mayer Reader
Midwinter Day
Carson McCullers, The Member of the Wedding
Thomas Merton, New Seeds of Contemplation
The Way of Chuang Tzu
Henri Michaux, A Barbarian in Asia
Dunya Mikhail, The Beekeeper
Henry Miller, The Colossus of Maroussi
Big Sur & the Oranges of Hieronymus Bosch
Yukio Mishima, Confessions of a Mask
Death in Midsummer
Star
Eugenio Montale, Selected Poems*
Vladimir Nabokov, Laughter in the Dark
Nikolai Gogol
The Real Life of Sebastian Knight
Pablo Neruda, The Captain's Verses*
Love Poems*
Charles Olson, Selected Writings
Mary Oppen, Meaning a Life
George Oppen, New Collected Poems
Wilfred Owen, Collected Poems
Hiroko Oyamada, The Factory
Michael Palmer, The Laughter of the Sphinx
Nicanor Parra, Antipoems*
Boris Pasternak, Safe Conduct
Kenneth Patchen
Memoirs of a Shy Pornographer
Octavio Paz, Poems of Octavio Paz
Victor Pelevin, Omon Ra
Alejandra Pizarnik
Extracting the Stone of Madness
Ezra Pound, The Cantos
New Selected Poems and Translations
Raymond Queneau, Exercises in Style
Qian Zhongshu, Fortress Besieged
Raja Rao, Kanthapura
Herbert Read, The Green Child
Kenneth Rexroth, Selected Poems
Keith Ridgway, Hawthorn & Child
Rainer Maria Rilke
Poems from the Book of Hours
Arthur Rimbaud, Illuminations*
A Season in Hell and The Drunken Boat*
Evelio Rosero, The Armies
Fran Ross, Oreo
Joseph Roth, The Emperor's Tomb
The Hotel Years
Raymond Roussel, Locus Solus
Ihara Saikaku, The Life of an Amorous Woman
Nathalie Sarraute, Tropisms
Jean-Paul Sartre, Nausea
Delmore Schwartz
In Dreams Begin Responsibilities
Hasan Shah, The Dancing Girl
W.G. Sebald, The Emigrants
The Rings of Saturn
Anne Serre, The Governesses
Stevie Smith, Best Poems
Gary Snyder, Turtle Island
Dag Solstad, Professor Andersen's Night
Muriel Spark, The Driver's Seat
Loitering with Intent
Antonio Tabucchi, Pereira Maintains
Junichiro Tanizaki, The Maids
Yoko Tawada, The Emissary
Memoirs of a Polar Bear
Dylan Thomas, A Child's Christmas in Wales
Collected Poems
Uwe Timm, The Invention of Curried Sausage
Tomas Tranströmer, The Great Enigma
Leonid Tsypkin, Summer in Baden-Baden
Tu Fu, Selected Poems
Paul Valéry, Selected Writings
Enrique Vila-Matas, Bartleby & Co.
Elio Vittorini, Conversations in Sicily
Rosmarie Waldrop, Gap Gardening
Robert Walser, The Assistant
The Tanners
The Walk
Eliot Weinberger, An Elemental Thing
The Ghosts of Birds
Nathanael West, The Day of the Locust
Miss Lonelyhearts
Tennessee Williams, The Glass Menagerie
A Streetcar Named Desire
William Carlos Williams, Selected Poems
Spring and All
Louis Zukofsky, "A"

*BILINGUAL EDITION

For a complete listing, request a free catalog from New Directions, 80 8th Avenue, New York, NY 10011 or visit us online at **ndbooks.com**